reflect ⁎ renovate ⁎ respond

renew

companion journal

Invite the Designer to Refresh Your Heart

Valerie Griffin

ISBN: 9781734675115

*Are you ready to refresh
the interior of your heart?*

**Enter in.
Renewal awaits you.**

How to Use This Journal

I am so excited for you to begin exploring renewal in a fresh way. The *Renew Companion Journal* provides space for you to reflect, renovate, and respond as you read *Renew: Invite the Designer to Refresh Your Heart* (available in print or digital format).

After each daily devotion in *Renew*, you will find a three-part application segment:

   • Reflect: This usually includes one or two additional scriptures to read, plus reflection questions.

   • Renovate: This delves deeper into your heart, exploring your thoughts, feelings, and what I sum up as "soul clutter."

   • Respond: This closing section consists of a prayer, listening to a song, or further reflection.

These three areas are listed in this journal with space to record your personal process of renewal. Additional Resources, available at valeriegriffin.com:

   • Weekly playlists
   • PDF worksheets
   • Scripture Cards

Reflect

Spend a few minutes thinking about when Christ first entered your life and began remodeling your heart.

What changes became visible as a result of your decision to follow Christ?

_____

_____

_____

_____

_____

_____

_____

_____

_____

_____

_____

_____

_____

_____

_____

_____

Renovate

Are you able to articulate your faith in Jesus and what He has done for you? Spend a few minutes writing out your story including as many details about the moment Jesus entered into your life as you can remember. Answering the following questions may help.

- Where were you?

- How old were you?

- Who was with you?

- Who helped you understand the gospel? What happened?

_____

_____

_____

_____

_____

_____

_____

_____

_____

_____

Respond

Pray for an opportunity this week to share your faith story.

You are being renewed in knowledge according to the image of your creator.

Colossians 3:10 CSB

Day 1: Architect of the Seasons

Reflect

Look out your window.

What evidence of renewal do you see?

_____

_____

_____

_____

_____

_____

Look within your heart.

What evidence of renewal do you see in your own life?

_____

_____

_____

_____

_____

_____

Read Habakkuk 3:2; Isaiah 42:5–9; Jeremiah 5:24; Acts 14:17.

Reflect on ways God has restored your relationships, replenished your strength, and revived your faith in him.

_____

_____

_____

_____

_____

_____

Renovate

Write down the weekly verse, Colossians 3:10, to memorize this week.

_____

_____

_____

_____

_____

_____

Respond

Listen to "Every Season" by Nichole Nordeman
(weekly playlists are available at valeriegriffin.com).

Day 2: The Designer of My Heart

Reflect

Read Psalm 13; Hebrews 3:4; John 15:15.

Acknowledge God as the Designer of your heart.

_____

_____

_____

_____

_____

_____

_____

_____

_____

_____

_____

_____

_____

_____

Renovate

Write a prayer to the Designer of your heart, requesting renewal.

_____

_____

_____

_____

_____

_____

_____

_____

_____

_____

Respond

Listen to "Beautiful Things" by Gungor.

Day 3: Schedule a Consultation

Reflect

Do you meet with God consistently?

_____

_____

What hinders you from approaching your heavenly Father?

Common hindrances include embarrassment/guilt, insecurities, self-reliance, busyness, or low priority.

_____

_____

_____

_____

_____

Do you believe God is good, loving, and trustworthy?

_____

_____

_____

_____

_____

_____

Read Jeremiah 33:3; Psalm 62:11–12; Psalm 91:1–2; Hebrews 11:6; 1 John 5:14–15.

Renovate

We seek God's help for many of the same reasons a client seeks a designer, but our hearts' Designer has limitless resources he makes available to us. Choose one or two of the following requests that resonate with you right now:

Guide me in my decisions. / Show me where to begin and what to focus on.

Remind me that you know the future. / Center my mind on your truth.

Assure me of your provision. / Deepen my trust in your sovereign plan.

Supply me with your attributes (love, grace, strength, peace, forgiveness, power, etc.).

_____

_____

_____

_____

_____

_____

_____

_____

_____

Respond

Now take those requests to God, spending time in prayer.

Loving God, you are the source of all I need. I praise you; you are loving, trustworthy, good, and all-powerful. You are all that I need, and yet I often allow _____ to hinder me from approaching you. Forgive me, Lord. Give me a deeper awareness of the things that stand in the way of me moving toward you. Grow my knowledge of you, my Creator. Amen.

Reflect

Read 1 Chronicles 29:11; Psalm 95:1–7; Psalm 99.

Renovate

Look up the definition of the word *bow*.

Evaluate your posture (of heart and body) before your King.

Respond

Close your eyes and imagine approaching the throne of Jesus, your loving King. See the details of royalty surrounding you. Magnificence beams in all directions as you humbly come before the Lord and make your request. What do you say to your King?

_____

_____

_____

_____

_____

_____

_____

_____

_____

_____

_____

_____

_____

_____

_____

_____

Day 5: Pushing Pause

Reflect

Read Psalm 62:1; Psalm 91:1–2; Philippians 4:8.

Close your eyes, quiet your heart, inhale and exhale slowly. Dwell on the character of God. If this is challenging for you, setting a timer may help.

Refrain from asking God for anything at this moment. Simply focus on who he is, either silently or audibly.

_____

_____

_____

_____

_____

_____

_____

_____

Renovate

Is there a specific area you need to "push pause" on a more regular basis? Some examples might be: negative thoughts, negative cultural influences, or people who bring you down.

_____

_____

_____

_____

_____

Write down your "area to pause from" and consider fasting for a specific time from that negative influence.

_____

_____

_____

_____

_____

_____

Respond

Where is your favorite place to be alone with God? A comfy chair? The kitchen table? Behind the wheel on your morning commute? On a path outdoors? Feet propped up while nestled into the sofa cushions? Perhaps you are there right now. Carve out some extra time in your schedule in the next day or two, so you can retreat to your quiet place. Listen to one of the following songs now, and save the titles to play at another time when you need an intentional pause.

- ✖ "Be Still My Soul" by Kari Jobe
- ✖ "I Want to Know You" by CityAlight
- ✖ "In the Secret of His Presence" by Sandra McCracken
- ✖ "Secret Place" by Phil Wickham

Weekly Reflection

This week we've looked at five facets of requesting renewal from the Designer of our hearts:

1. Season after season, God guides his creation in transformation.
2. The Designer of my heart is the only One capable of renewing my heart.
3. Consistent consultations with my Designer sustain the process of renewal.
4. Requesting renewal requires a posture of humility.
5. Pausing to acknowledge God is an act of worship.

Reflect

In what ways did you grow in understanding of God and yourself this week?

_____

_____

Which scripture was especially meaningful to you?

_____

_____

_____

_____

Respond

Choose one truth, verse, or personal reflection to share with a friend.

_____

_____

_____

_____

Rhythm of Renewal

We have finished our first letter (R) in the acronym RENEW. This section provides a place to review each weekly letter as we build our acronym.

REQUEST RENEWAL

King of Kings, you are my source for renewal. I recognize my deep need for you and acknowledge I am unable to revive my heart. Please renew me in knowledge according to your image, as your word says in Colossians 3:10. I request renewal from you, the Designer of my heart. Amen.

Create in me a clean heart,
O God, and renew
a right spirit within me.

Psalm 51:10 ESV

Reflect

Read Romans 7:15-20.

Can you relate to Paul? In what ways?

_____

_____

_____

_____

_____

_____

_____

_____

Renovate

Last week we asked God, the Designer, to renew our hearts from a posture of humility. This week, we are going to roll up our sleeves and tackle soul clutter. As with any home design project, we must first evaluate the contents before clarifying the changes we hope to see.

Today we begin our Soul Clutter inventory.

Soul Clutter is anything that fills your mind and heart—decisions, delights, demands, difficulties, dilemmas, disappointments, dreams, and duties.

Like the papers strewn over my counter, we need to look at our heart clutter—really see and name it—before we can sort through it. Spend five to seven minutes naming the thoughts scattered across your mind. List them on your *Soul Clutter* page. Don't write how you feel about these thoughts, simply jot down everything filling your mind at the moment in the space provided. Use additional sheets if needed. We'll be referring back to our *Soul Clutter* all week, so you'll complete the *Sort It Out* sheet later.

Respond

Write down the weekly verse, Psalm 51:10, to memorize this week.

_____

_____

_____

_____

_____

_____

_____

Soul Clutter

Soul Clutter is anything that fills your mind and heart—decisions, delights, demands, difficulties, dilemmas, disappointments, dreams, and duties. Spend five to seven minutes naming the thoughts scattered across your mind. Don't write how you feel about these thoughts, simply jot down everything filling your mind at the moment in the space provided.

Sort It Out

Day 2

Thought: _____

This makes me feel _____

_____

because _____

_____

_____

_____

_____

Day 3

sin(s) uncovered:

_____

_____

_____

_____

_____

_____

_____

_____

_____

Day 4

unbelief(s) exposed:

_____

_____

_____

_____

_____

_____

_____

Day 5

prayer for repentance:

_____

_____

_____

_____

_____

_____

_____

_____

Day 2: Our Helper

Reflect

How often do you feel alone physically, emotionally, or spiritually?

_____

_____

_____

_____

Read John 14:16. This passage tells us we are never alone. The Holy Spirit helps us and provides truth to make sense of our thoughts and feelings.

Now read Psalm 28:7, Psalm 68:19, and 1 Peter 5:7. Spend a few moments quietly meditating on these truths, recognizing God's presence with you.

_____

_____

_____

_____

_____

_____

_____

Renovate

Prayerfully look at your *Soul Clutter* page from yesterday. Place a star beside thoughts that are heavy or prominent on your mind right now—things that are weighing you down or filling your mental capacity.

Choose one thought that you starred, and write it on the *Sort It Out* page.
Then complete the following sentence: This makes me feel _____
because_____.

I encourage you to be honest and delve into the root of your feelings. Naming our emotions brings clarity. Moving our thoughts onto a page, then sorting through the emotions attached to them helps us know what to do with those thoughts (we'll get to that tomorrow).

_____

_____

_____

_____

_____

_____

_____

_____

_____

Respond

Listen to "Lay It All Down" by Will Reagan, United Pursuit.

Day 3: The Uncovering

Reflect

Let's ask the Holy Spirit to remove the excuses, justifications, or indifference we've used to cover our sins.

In the process, know that not all soul clutter is wrong. We have thoughts, actions, and feelings that fill our hearts but are not sinful. Celebrate the good things as you expose your shortcomings.

_____

_____

_____

_____

_____

_____

_____

_____

_____

Renovate

Looking at the feelings you wrote down yesterday on your *Sort It Out* page, what thoughts, words, or actions have those feelings produced that are displeasing to God?

_____

_____

_____

_____

Ask the Holy Spirit to uncover the sin in your heart, and list them beside "sin(s) uncovered." You may want to refer to the table below or the passage in Ephesians 4:17–32.

Sin	Excuse	Scripture
Fear	*This threatens my comfort, my people, my plans, my opinions, my future.*	Isaiah 41:10
Selfishness	*I don't have the time, energy, money, capacity for (fill in the blank).*	Philippians 2:3
Entitlement	*I deserve it!*	Philippians 4:12
Impatience	*I reacted negatively because…my personality type, lack of sleep, (fill in the blank).*	Proverbs 19:11
Control	*I want my plans to unfold for my life (and the lives of my people).*	Psalm 9:10

Spend some time in prayer confessing any sin you've uncovered, and thank Jesus for his gift of kindness and forgiveness (Romans 2:4).

_____

_____

_____

_____

_____

_____

_____

Respond

Listen to "Out of Hiding (Father's Song)" by Steffany Gretzinger and Amanda Lindsey Cook.

Reflect

In scripture, God lays out a detailed plan for us to have an abundant life with him. Do you believe him?

_____

_____

_____

_____

Renovate

Ask God to expose areas of unbelief, using the table on the following page for reference.

_____

_____

_____

_____

_____

Refer to your *Sort It Out* page. Do any of your thoughts or attitudes uncover a lack of faith?

List struggles of unbelief next to "unbelief(s) exposed."

_____

_____

_____

_____

I believe *God's...*

identity		capability	
God is good	Ps. 25:8; 119:68	God forgives	Ps. 103; 65:3; John 3:16
God is loving	Rom. 5:8; 1 John 4:16	God restores	Ps. 51:12; 80:3; Rev. 21:5
God is holy	1 Sam. 2:2; Isa. 6:3; Ps. 99	God provides	Lam. 3:22-23; 2 Pet. 1:3
God is mighty	Job 9:4; 26:7-11; Ps. 150:2	God triumphs	John 16:33; 1 Cor. 15:54-57
God is sovereign	Jer. 29:11; Col. 1:16-17; Rom. 11:36	God strengthens	Ps. 59:17; Isa. 41:10; 2 Cor. 12:9; 1 Pet. 5:10

I believe *my...*

identity		capability	
I am loved	Rom. 8:31-39; Eph. 3:16-19	To glorify God	Eph. 3:20-21; Phil. 2:13
I am forgiven	Col. 2:13-14; 1 John 4:10	To love others	Lev. 19:18; 1 Pet. 4:8
I am God's child	John 1:12-13; Gal. 4:4-7	To serve others	Gal. 5:13-14; 1 Pet. 4:9-10
I am a work of art	Gen. 1:27, 31; Ps. 139:13-16	To forgive others	Eph. 4:32; Col. 3:12-13
I am fully known	1 Kings 8:39; Ps. 56:8; Ps. 139; Matt. 10:30	To rest in Christ	Matt. 11:28-30; Phil. 4:6-9, 11-13; John 14:27

I believe *the Bible's...*

identity		capability	
God's Word	1 Thess. 2:13; 2 Tim. 3:16	To teach me	Ps. 119; Rom. 15:4; 2 Tim. 3:15-16
A guiding light	Ps. 119:105; 2 Pet. 1:19-21	To discern my heart	Heb. 4:12; Ps. 119:11
An eternal narrative	Heb. 4:12; Jn. 6:63	To work within me	Col. 3:16; Eph. 6:17
The Truth	Jn. 17:17; 2 Sam. 7:28	To accomplish God's purpose	Isa. 55:11; Matt. 4:4
The story of redemption	Genesis through Revelation	To declare the Gospel	Luke 24:45-47; John 5:39

Respond

Listen to "Who You Say I Am" by Hillsong Worship.

Day 5: Light for the Heart

Reflect

Read John 1:9; John 8:12; John 12:46.

Meditate on Jesus as the Light of your heart.

_____

_____

_____

_____

_____

Renovate

This week, we have used the following scripture to help us evaluate soul clutter:

> When He arrives, He will uncover the sins of the world, expose unbelief as sin, and allow all to **see their sins in light of righteousness** for the first time. (*John 16:8–9, emphasis added*)

The Holy Spirit helps us evaluate soul clutter by uncovering sin, exposing unbelief as sin, and allowing us to see our sins in light of perfection.

Refer to your ***Sort It Out*** page. Ask the Spirit to help you see your faults in light of God's holiness, as you write a prayer of repentance.

_____

_____

_____

_____

_____

_____

_____

_____

_____

_____

Respond

Jesus, You are perfect, holy, righteous. You walked this broken world, experiencing life as a human and responded perfectly to every situation. I fall so short of this, Lord. Forgive me for ignoring and downplaying my sin. Forgive me for using others as a means of comparing my soul. You are the standard, Jesus, and you are perfect. I desire a renewed heart. Help me see the broken places within me, which only you can restore. Thank you for the cross and daily grace to follow you. Amen.

Weekly Reflection

This week we've looked at five facets of evaluating soul clutter:

1. Feeling overwhelmed indicates my cluttered soul needs attention.
2. The Holy Spirit helps me sort through soul clutter.
3. The Spirit helps me uncover my sin.
4. Renewal requires believing God.
5. The light of Jesus illuminates my heart.

Reflect

In what ways did you grow in understanding of God and yourself this week?

_____

_____

_____

_____

Which scripture was especially meaningful to you?

_____

_____

_____

_____

Respond

Choose one truth, verse, or personal reflection to share with a friend.

_____

_____

_____

_____

Rhythm of Renewal

This section provides a place to review each letter as we build our acronym.

REQUEST RENEWAL

Spend a few moments quieting your heart and request renewal.

EVALUATE SOUL CLUTTER

God, I echo the words of the children's song: You are so big, so strong, and so mighty—there's nothing you cannot do. You are capable of de-cluttering my heart. Help me sort through my soul clutter, deepen my belief in you, and see my sin in light of your righteousness. Amen.

*Let your minds on
things above,
not on earthly things.*

Colossians 3:2 CSB

Reflect

Read the Psalm 18:19; Psalm 31:8; Psalm 118:5.

Reflect on God's gracious ability to bring you into a spacious place of freedom.

_____

_____

_____

_____

_____

Renovate

Consider how soul clutter makes you claustrophobic. How do you feel after sorting through your thoughts last week?

_____

_____

_____

_____

_____

_____

_____

_____

Choose one or two suggestions from the list to add white space to your week.

_____

_____

_____

_____

_____

Respond

Write down the weekly verse, Colossians 3:2, to memorize this week.

_____

_____

_____

_____

_____

Listen to "Open Space" by Housefires.

Reflect

When you are at the end of your life, what would you like others to remember about you?

_____

_____

_____

_____

_____

Take an honest look at your life. What is your focus on?

_____

_____

_____

_____

_____

_____

Renovate

Last week, we sorted soul clutter, but unfortunately, clutter will continue to accumulate. Let's be mindful of the focus of our thoughts this week and look for patterns of wrong or negative thinking.

What is on your mind right now? A worry, a fear, a disappointment? Write them down. Take one or two of your pressing thoughts and pinpoint the focus. Then take those thoughts to Jesus, asking him to align your vision with his.

Respond

Listen to "Build My Life" by Housefires.

Day 3: The Design Plan

Reflect

Read Jeremiah 29:11; Psalm 143:5; 2 Corinthians 5:17.

Spend a few moments thanking God for his good plan for your life.

_____

_____

_____

_____

_____

_____

_____

_____

_____

_____

Renovate

Consider the interior of your heart. Is there anything that distracts, blurs, or opposes God's design for your life?

_____

_____

_____

_____

_____

What is one step you can take today to zoom in on heavenly things instead of earthly things?

_____

_____

_____

_____

_____

_____

_____

_____

Respond

Sing or read the following hymn in worship.

"Be Thou My Vision"

Be Thou my Vision, O Lord of my heart; Naught be all else to me, save that Thou art— Thou my best thought, by day or by night, Waking or sleeping, Thy presence my light.

Be Thou my Wisdom, and Thou my true Word; I ever with Thee and Thou with me, Lord; Thou my great Father, I Thy true son, Thou in me dwelling, and I with Thee one.

Riches I heed not, nor man's empty praise, Thou mine inheritance, now and always; Thou and Thou only, first in my heart, High King of heaven, my Treasure Thou art.

High King of heaven, my victory won, May I reach heaven's joys, O bright heav'n's Sun! Heart of my own heart, whate'er befall, Still be my Vision, O Ruler of all.

Day 4: Mirrors of Reflection

Reflect

Meditate on 2 Corinthians 3:18.

How are you reflecting the Lord to those in your sphere of influence?

_____

_____

_____

_____

_____

_____

_____

In what ways do you desire to reflect Jesus more clearly?

_____

_____

_____

_____

_____

_____

_____

_____

Renovate

Refer to your *Soul Clutter* page. Consider how God may be using the things you listed to transform you.

How might your responses to the situations listed either reflect Jesus or obscure your reflection of him?

_____

_____

_____

_____

_____

_____

_____

_____

_____

_____

_____

_____

Respond

Spend some time in prayer, remembering that it is the Spirit of the Lord who accomplishes his work within you.

Reflect

What circumstances have contributed to the pattern of perspective with which you view life?

_____

_____

_____

_____

_____

Are there tendencies or triggers that negatively obscure your view?

_____

_____

_____

_____

_____

On a scale of 1-10, how would you rate your "soul's window covering" in viewing the world from your unique, yet biblical perspective?

_____

_____

_____

_____

_____

Renovate

Glance at your *Soul Clutter* page. Of the things on your list, is your perspective hindering or helping you see the situation from a biblical viewpoint?

_____

_____

_____

_____

_____

_____

_____

_____

_____

_____

_____

Respond

God, help me to make you—not the temporary things of my life—my focal point. Guide me with your Word and deepen my understanding of you and how you want me to live. You have given me a unique perspective, but I don't want my view of things to hinder me from growing closer to you. Thank you for your grace when my heart gets distracted. Be my Vision, and change me according to your plan for my life. Amen.

Weekly Reflection

This week we've looked at five facets of narrowing our focus on Jesus:

1. The clarity of white space brings awareness of my spiritual needs.
2. Without a clear focus on Jesus, I lose sight of my purpose.
3. I implement God's Design Plan by growing in my knowledge of him through scripture.
4. God desires to transform my heart to reflect his brilliant glory.
5. The changes God makes within me reframe my view of life.

Reflect

In what ways did you grow in understanding of God and yourself this week?

_____

_____

_____

_____

Which scripture was especially meaningful to you?

_____

_____

_____

_____

Respond

Choose one truth, verse, or personal reflection to share with a friend.

_____

_____

_____

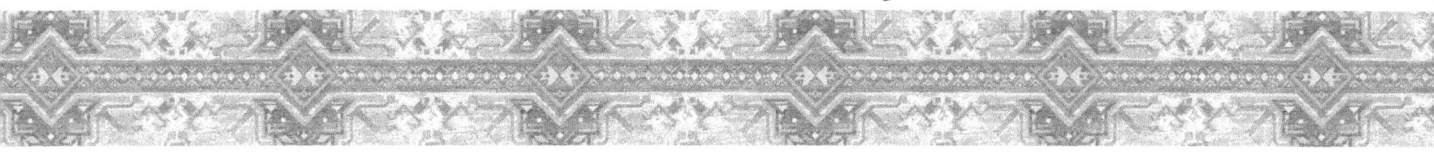

Rhythm of Renewal

This section provides a place to review each letter as we build our acronym.

REQUEST RENEWAL

Spend a few moments quieting your heart and request renewal.

EVALUATE SOUL CLUTTER

What thoughts are filling your mind right now?

NARROW YOUR FOCUS

Jesus, it's all about you, not me. I desire you to be the main focus of my life. Please forgive my tendencies to shift my view of you and your ways into my periphery. Raise my gaze to stay on you today. Amen.

Do not conform to the pattern of this world, but be transformed by the renewing of your mind. Then you will be able to test and approve what God's will is—his good, pleasing and perfect will.

Romans 12:2 NIV

Reflect

Read Psalm 19:8; Psalm 119:105; 2 Corinthians 4:6.

How has God illuminated a situation in your life through scripture?

_____

_____

_____

_____

_____

_____

Renovate

Refer to your *Soul Clutter* page. Do you see evidence of God using anything on your list to become a light? This could be a good, neutral, or negative item—God uses it all.

Ask God to illuminate areas in your heart that you haven't seen before. As Corrie ten Boom said, "Let God's promises shine on your problems."

_____

_____

_____

_____

_____

_____

_____

_____

_____

_____

_____

_____

Respond

Write down the weekly verse, Romans 12:2, to memorize this week.

_____

_____

_____

_____

_____

_____

Listen to "Your Word" by Hillsong.

Day 2: Hues of Holiness

Reflect

Peruse the palette of your soul, using the table on the next page.

What hues are part of your color scheme?

_____

_____

_____

_____

_____

Are there any colors you would like to see more of in your life?

_____

_____

_____

_____

Renovate

Choose one color from the *Hues of Holiness* table to focus on over the next several weeks.

Be mindful of noticing the hue as you go about your day, reminding you to choose the color quality (love, cheerfulness, hope, peace, etc) in your daily thoughts and interactions with others.

_____

_____

_____

Hues of Holiness

Red	Love for others because of the love Jesus poured out for you on the cross	Romans 5:5-8 John 15:12
Pink	Contagious cheerfulness because you enjoy the faithful companionship of God	Psalm 16
Orange	Zeal for living this abundant life well	Romans 12:11 John 10:10
Yellow	Eternal hope that shines the light of Jesus	Isaiah 60:19-20
Green	Refreshing righteousness as you follow your Shepherd	Psalm 23
Turquoise	Deep reservoirs of resolve to find satisfaction in God alone	Psalm 63
Blue	Peace in the storm as you hold fast to Jesus, your anchor	John 4:14 John 14:27 John 16:33
Purple	Kingdom-minded purpose because you are a child of the King	1 Peter 2:9-12

Respond

Thank God for his gift of colors in creation, and ask him to use his hues of holiness within your heart.

_____

_____

_____

_____

Reflect

Read the weekly verse, Romans 12:2.

How has God transformed you by renewing your mind?

_____

_____

_____

_____

What worldly patterns have you discontinued in your life?

_____

_____

_____

_____

_____

Renovate

Refer to your *Soul Clutter* page and spend some time reflecting on your mind and heart. Use the list below to evaluate the patterns in your heart.

Patterns of this World or Patterns of Righteousness:

* Selfishness or Service (Mark 10:45)
* Pride or Humility (Philippians 2:3)
* Rush or Rest (Psalm 39:6; Matthew 11:28)
* Worry or Trust (Philippians 4:6; Proverbs 3:5)
* Greed or Generosity (Luke 12:33)

Respond

Ask God to renew your mind by transforming any pattern that does not align with his ways. It may be helpful to choose one pattern and supporting scripture at a time to focus on.

Reflect

Read Psalm 138:7–8; Romans 8:18; 1 Peter 5:10.

Reflect on the comfortable and uncomfortable textures of circumstances in your life.

Are there any painful patches in your past where you see God's plan becoming more visible?

Renovate

Look over your *Soul Clutter* page. What situations are uncomfortable or painful for you?

Spend some time telling God how you feel, then ask him for strength to endure.

Respond

Listen to one of the following songs now, and save the titles to play at another time when you need a reminder God is sovereign over your circumstance.

- ✖ "Raise A Hallelujah" by Bethel Music
- ✖ "Sovereign Over Us" by Michael W. Smith
- ✖ "Give Me Faith" by Elevation Worship
- ✖ "Trust in You" by Lauren Daigle
- ✖ "It Is Well with My Soul" by Audrey Assad

Reflect

In what areas or circumstances of your life do you feel God has given you a unique design to showcase his glory?

_____

_____

_____

_____

_____

_____

_____

Renovate

Using decorating vocabulary, write a few sentences describing one area you listed above, describing how God is layering the following elements in your heart:

- Light of Scripture
- Hues of Holiness
- Patterns of Righteousness
- Smooth/Rough Textures of Circumstance

_____

_____

_____

_____

Are you resisting any of the above elements in your heart?

_____

_____

_____

Respond

Close by reading the following verse, making it your prayer today:

"Let the word of the Anointed One richly inhabit your lives" (Colossians 3:16).

_____

_____

_____

_____

_____

Lord, you are a great and gracious God. You carry out your good plan for my life in generous and tender ways. Thank you for using hues of holiness, patterns of righteousness, textures of circumstances, and the light of scripture to transform my heart. I confess my resistance to your methods of remaking my soul's interior, yet I know your design is better than any I can envision. Revive me with your words, Jesus. Speak to me throughout my day—that your word may richly inhabit my life. Layer your holy elements within my heart, Lord. Amen.

Weekly Reflection

This week we've looked at five design elements of the heart:

1. The light of scripture illuminates my life.
2. The canvas of my life displays hues of God's holiness.
3. I need to routinely evaluate the patterns residing in my mind.
4. God weaves difficulties into a masterful design I cannot fully see.
5. My skilled Creator layers heart elements in a beautiful unique-to-me design.

Reflect

In what ways did you grow in understanding of God and yourself this week?

_____

_____

_____

_____

Which scripture was especially meaningful to you?

_____

_____

_____

_____

Respond

Choose one truth, verse, or personal reflection to share with a friend.

_____

_____

_____

Rhythm of Renewal

This section provides a place to review each letter as we build our acronym.

REQUEST RENEWAL

Spend a few moments quieting your heart and request renewal.

EVALUATE SOUL CLUTTER

What thoughts are filling your mind right now?

NARROW YOUR FOCUS

What is the focus of your most pressing thoughts?

EQUIP WITH TRUTH

God, you are a creative and masterful Designer. I stand in awe of how you curate my circumstances, relationships, and faith into a design beyond my comprehension. Thank you for starting the work of renewal in my heart and promising to complete it. Continue to equip my heart with truth to display your glory. Amen.

*The beauty of faith-filled
people encompasses me.
They are true, and my heart
is thrilled beyond measure.*

Psalm 16:3

Reflect

Do you regularly worship with other believers? Why or why not?

_____

_____

_____

_____

Have you experienced renewal as a result of going to church? If so, in what ways?

_____

_____

_____

_____

_____

_____

_____

Renovate

Think of a time when you experienced the glory of heaven surrounded by other believers. Describe the setting, your feelings, and the details of the experience.

_____

_____

_____

_____

_____

_____

_____

_____

_____

_____

_____

_____

Respond

Write down the weekly verse in the translation below to memorize this week:

"The beauty of faith-filled people encompasses me. They are true, and my heart is thrilled beyond measure" (Psalm 16:3).

_____

_____

_____

_____

_____

_____

_____

_____

Send a note to someone in your church who you appreciate.

Day 2: Place of Authentic Love

Reflect

Read the following scripture:

"Love others well, and don't hide behind a mask; love authentically. Despise evil; pursue what is good as if your life depends on it" (Romans 12:9).

Do you believe authenticity can be a way to show love? How?

_____

_____

_____

_____

_____

_____

_____

_____

_____

_____

_____

Renovate

What masks (or filters presenting perfection) do you have a tendency to hide behind?

_____

_____

_____

_____

What relationships in your life are authentic, where you welcome others in to see the real you?

_____

_____

_____

_____

_____

_____

_____

_____

_____

_____

_____

_____

Respond

Think of one person who you'd like to get to know better. Schedule coffee or a phone call to connect with authenticity.

Reflect

Have you ever experienced the *openness + vulnerability = comfort* equation? What insight do you have from that experience?

_____

_____

_____

Read Proverbs 11:25. How have you experienced refreshment from others?

_____

_____

_____

_____

_____

_____

Renovate

How comfortable are you opening the door to your heart?

_____

_____

_____

_____

_____

What does the welcome mat of your heart say?

- ✖ "I'm fine, no soliciting."
- ✖ "I'm a wreck, come on in!"
- ✖ Or somewhere in between, depending on who is at your door?

_____

_____

_____

_____

_____

_____

Respond

Practice hospitality: pray for a friend who is experiencing difficulty right now.

_____

_____

_____

_____

_____

_____

Practice vulnerability: tell a friend about a struggle or stress you are experiencing.

Day 4: Speak Truth in Love

Reflect

Who are the friends in your life who have sharpened you?

_____

_____

_____

How has God used you in a friend's life?

_____

_____

_____

Renovate

Re-read the list below from Proverbs. What areas do you feel God has equipped you to sharpen others?

- �֎ Sharpen me with wise counsel (Proverbs 27:9)
- ✖ Love me through thick and thin (Proverbs 17:17)
- ✖ Forgive and be forgiven (Proverbs 17:9)
- ✖ Listen with calmness (Proverbs 17:27)
- ✖ Speak life-giving words (Proverbs 10:11)
- ✖ Offer words that remove the weight of worry (Proverbs 12:25)
- ✖ Serve nourishing conversation (Proverbs 18:20)
- ✖ Extinguish gossip (Proverbs 26:20)

_____

_____

_____

_____

Are there any areas of "sharpening" you'd like to grow in?

_____

_____

_____

_____

_____

Respond

Thank God for your life-giving friendships and ask him for opportunities to extend the grace of friendship to others.

_____

_____

_____

_____

_____

Listen to "Blessed Be the Tie" by Sara Groves.

Reflect

Read the following verses:

"Whenever you cross my mind, I thank my God for you and for the gift of knowing you. My spirit is lightened with joy whenever I pray for you" (Philippians 1:3–4).

Who came to your mind as you read this passage?

_____

_____

_____

_____

_____

_____

Renovate

List the names of your closest friends.

_____

_____

_____

Now, write how your faith has grown because of their friendship. How has God shown you more of himself through them?

_____

_____

_____

_____

_____

_____

_____

_____

_____

How can you encourage your friends to live out their unique God-given design?
Consider sending them a note, text, or email of encouragement.

_____

_____

_____

_____

_____

_____

Respond

Pray specifically for each of your friends, using the words of Paul:

"Father, may their love grow more and more in wisdom and insight—so they will be able to examine and determine the best from everything else. And on the day of the Anointed One, the day of His judgment, let them stand pure and blameless, filled with the fruit of righteousness that ripens through Jesus the Anointed. All this I pray, with a view to God's ultimate praise and glory" (Philippians 1:9). Amen.

Weekly Reflection

This week we've looked at five aspects of welcoming others into our hearts:

1. The weekly practice of corporate worship recharges our souls.

2. We reflect Christ's love when we shed the attempted illusion of perfection, welcoming others in with authenticity.

3. Heart hospitality is opening yourself to vulnerability and welcoming others into a place of comfort.

4. God places people in our lives to help our faith develop with greater clarity, distinction, and definition.

5. Good friends help us live out God's design for our lives.

Reflect

In what ways did you grow in understanding of God and yourself this week?

_____

_____

_____

_____

Which scripture was especially meaningful to you?

_____

_____

_____

_____

Respond

Choose one truth, verse, or personal reflection to share with a friend.

_____

_____

Rhythm of Renewal

This section provides a place to review each letter as we build our acronym.

REQUEST RENEWAL

Spend a few moments quieting your heart and request renewal.

EVALUATE SOUL CLUTTER

What thoughts are filling your mind right now?

NARROW YOUR FOCUS

What is the focus of your most pressing thoughts?

EQUIP WITH TRUTH

What truth do you need to furnish your heart?

WELCOME OTHERS IN

Jesus, thank you for enriching my life with friends. In the words of David from Psalm 16:3, "The beauty of faith-filled people encompasses me." Show me ways to bless and encourage my friends. Give me the courage and wisdom to be vulnerable. Continue to use friendships to show me more of your character and deepen my faith. Amen.

Therefore we do not lose heart. Though outwardly we are wasting away, yet inwardly we are being renewed day by day.

2 Corinthians 4:16 NIV

Reflect

What emotions does the phrase *ongoing renewal* generate in your mind? Some examples might be discouragement, hope, fear, or thankfulness. Why do you feel this way?

_____

_____

_____

_____

_____

_____

_____

Read the following verse: *"So we do not lose heart. Though our outer self is wasting away, our inner self is being renewed day by day"* *(2 Corinthians 4:16 ESV).*

How does this truth encourage you?

_____

_____

_____

_____

_____

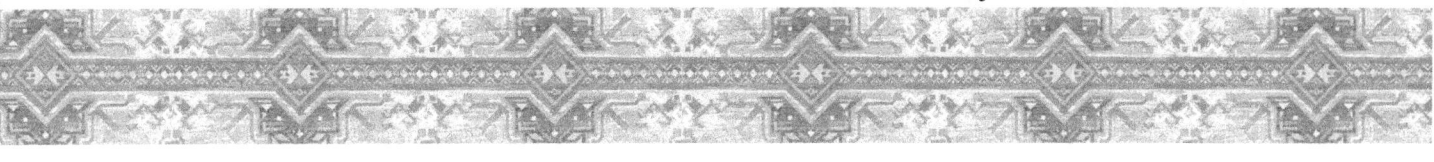

Renovate

This week, instead of having a *Renovate* section, we will focus on our acronym (see note below under *Rhythm of Renewal*).

Respond

Write down the weekly scripture, 2 Corinthians 4:16, to memorize this week.

_____

_____

_____

_____

_____

Rhythm of Renewal

We have been building on our acronym RENEW for five weeks. Renewal doesn't end on the last page of this devotional—it continues every day God gives us life on earth.

This acronym review section is included on each day of this week so that we can practice the rhythm of renewal daily. My prayer is that after you finish this devotional, you will continue inviting the Designer of your heart to renew you.

You may want to begin a new *Soul Clutter* page this week, and renovate areas we covered in previous weeks. Use this section to best serve your needs each day.

Day 1: One Glory to Another

Request Renewal

Spend a few moments quieting your heart and request renewal.

Evaluate Soul Clutter

What thoughts are filling your mind right now?

_____

_____

_____

_____

_____

_____

Narrow Your Focus

What is the focus of your most pressing thoughts?

_____

_____

_____

_____

_____

_____

Equip With Truth

What truth do you need to furnish your heart?

Welcome Others In

What is one area of heart hospitality you'd like to practice more?

Day 2: Leave it to The Professional

Reflect

Read Colossians 2:6–7.

Do you struggle with relinquishing control to the Lord? If so, in what areas of your life is this particularly challenging?

_____

_____

_____

_____

_____

_____

_____

Where has God demonstrated more knowledge, capability, tools, experience, or vision than you did?

_____

_____

_____

_____

_____

Respond

Listen to "Take My Life" by Chris Tomlin.

Rhythm of Renewal

Request Renewal

Spend a few moments quieting your heart and request renewal.

Evaluate Soul Clutter

What thoughts are filling your mind right now?

_____

_____

_____

_____

_____

_____

_____

Narrow Your Focus

What is the focus of your most pressing thoughts?

_____

_____

_____

_____

_____

_____

_____

Equip With Truth

What truth do you need to furnish your heart?

_____

_____

_____

_____

_____

_____

_____

Welcome Others In

What is one area of heart hospitality you'd like to practice more?

_____

_____

_____

_____

_____

Reflect

As you've explored your heart the past five weeks, have you found unexpected sin?

_____

_____

_____

_____

_____

_____

_____

_____

_____

How have your scars brought God glory?

_____

_____

_____

_____

_____

_____

_____

_____

_____

_____

_____

_____

_____

_____

_____

_____

_____

_____

_____

_____

_____

Respond

Listen to "Sovereign Over Us" by Michael W. Smith.

Rhythm of Renewal

Request Renewal

Spend a few moments quieting your heart and request renewal.

Evaluate Soul Clutter

What thoughts are filling your mind right now?

_____

_____

_____

_____

_____

_____

Narrow Your Focus

What is the focus of your most pressing thoughts?

_____

_____

_____

_____

_____

_____

Equip With Truth

What truth do you need to furnish your heart?

Welcome Others In

What is one area of heart hospitality you'd like to practice more?

Reflect

Spend time thanking God for His fingerprints of renewal on your life and the world around you.

_____

_____

_____

_____

_____

_____

_____

_____

_____

_____

_____

_____

_____

_____

_____

_____

_____

Respond

Listen to "Everything" by TobyMac (dance party is optional, but encouraged).

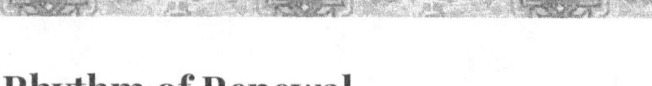

Rhythm of Renewal

Request Renewal

Spend a few moments quieting your heart and request renewal.

Evaluate Soul Clutter

What thoughts are filling your mind right now?

_____

_____

_____

_____

_____

_____

Narrow Your Focus

What is the focus of your most pressing thoughts?

_____

_____

_____

_____

_____

_____

Equip With Truth

What truth do you need to furnish your heart?

_____

_____

_____

_____

_____

_____

_____

Welcome Others In

What is one area of heart hospitality you'd like to practice more?

_____

_____

_____

_____

_____

Reflect

Consider all the details God is orchestrating on your behalf. In what circumstances have you seen evidence of his creativity, his restoration, his timing, and his goodness?

_____

_____

_____

_____

_____

_____

_____

_____

_____

_____

_____

_____

_____

_____

_____

Spend some time meditating on your heavenly home while reading the following scriptures:

2 Timothy 4:18; Hebrews 12:22–24; 2 Peter 3:13–15;
Revelation 5:11–14; Revelation 21:1–8; Revelation 22:1-5.

_____

_____

_____

_____

_____

_____

_____

Respond

God, season after season, you guide creation in transformation. Along with all nature and animals and microscopic life hidden from eyes, you created me. Renew me in knowledge according to your image, God. I acknowledge that you are the Designer of my heart. I am wonderfully made because you, the Creator, are wonderful. Forgive me for attempting DIY projects to grow spiritually. You said, Jesus, that apart from you I can do nothing. So once again, I relinquish control to you. Thank you for the gift of renewal—for supplying new mercies daily to encourage me in this walk of faith. Jesus, thank you for entering into this broken world and showing all of humanity perfect love. Your death and resurrection gave me the key to enter my eternal home with you. Until that day, renew me. I invite you—the Designer—to continue refreshing my heart in an ongoing rhythm of renewal until the day you welcome me home. Amen.

Rhythm of Renewal

Request Renewal

Spend a few moments quieting your heart and request renewal.

Evaluate Soul Clutter

What thoughts are filling your mind right now?

_____

_____

_____

_____

_____

_____

Narrow Your Focus

What is the focus of your most pressing thoughts?

_____

_____

_____

_____

_____

_____

Equip With Truth

What truth do you need to furnish your heart?

_____

_____

_____

_____

_____

_____

Welcome Others In

What is one area of heart hospitality you'd like to practice more?

_____

_____

_____

_____

_____

Weekly Reflection

This week we've looked at five facets of the cycle of renewal:

1. My heart needs God's intervention day after day.
2. Instead of DIY-ing my renewal, I leave it to Jesus.
3. In the middle of the mess, I remember Jesus.
4. My Creator leaves fingerprints of renewal on everything he touches.
5. Through faith alone in Christ alone, I will be welcomed home.

Reflect

In what ways did you grow in understanding of God and yourself this week?

_____

_____

_____

_____

Which scripture was especially meaningful to you?

_____

_____

_____

_____

Respond

Choose one truth, verse, or personal reflection to share with a friend.

_____

_____

_____

_____

Rhythm of Renewal

This section provides a place to review each letter as we build our acronym.

REQUEST RENEWAL

Spend a few moments quieting your heart and request renewal.

EVALUATE SOUL CLUTTER

What thoughts are filling your mind right now?

NARROW YOUR FOCUS

What is the focus of your most pressing thoughts?

EQUIP WITH TRUTH

What truth do you need to furnish your heart?

WELCOME OTHERS IN

What is one area of heart hospitality you'd like to practice more?

THE CYCLE OF RENEWAL

God, you are Creator, Designer, Redeemer, and Restorer. You are always the same because you are God, yet you don't leave me the same—because your plan for me is better than my plan. You are making all things new, including my heart. Continue to renew me in your way for your glory until the day I am home with you. Amen.

Sort It Out

Day 2

Thought: _____

This makes me feel _____

_____

because _____

_____

_____

_____

_____

Day 3

sin(s) uncovered:

_____

_____

_____

_____

_____

_____

_____

_____

_____

_____

Day 4

unbelief(s) exposed:

_____
_____
_____
_____
_____
_____
_____
_____

Day 5

prayer for repentance:

_____
_____
_____
_____
_____
_____
_____
_____

Sort It Out

Day 2

Thought: _____

This makes me feel _____

_____

because _____

_____

_____

_____

Day 3

sin(s) uncovered:

_____

_____

_____

_____

_____

_____

_____

_____

_____

Day 4

unbelief(s) exposed:

_____

_____

_____

_____

_____

_____

_____

_____

Day 5

prayer for repentance:

_____

_____

_____

_____

_____

_____

_____

_____

CPSIA information can be obtained
at www.ICGtesting.com
Printed in the USA
BVHW011726110820
586125BV00004B/68

9 781734 675115